Elves Can't
DUNK

Robert Skead

Tale Blazer Productions
Elves Can't Dunk
Copyright ©2016 by Robert Skead
www.robertskead.com
Library of Congress Cataloging in Publication Data in Progress.

Sebastian decides to prove himself by trying out for his favorite professional basketball team. There's just one small problem–Sebastian is an elf at the North Pole. And elves can't dunk! To solve this dunking dilemma, Sebastian takes some of Santa's magic feed corn–the stuff that makes his reindeer fly–to his tryout for the team. This corn will give Sebastian more hang time than Michael Jordan on the moon! When Sebastian's idol, Coach Tanner, discovers the corn, he begins to dream of his own championships for his team of losers. Tanner sets out on a mission to steal the corn from Santa and it's up to Sebastian and his best friends to catch him and save Christmas!

ISBN: 978-0-9907666-3-6 (paperback)

Cover Design: Ray Nelson
Illustrations by Kyle Holveck and Aaron Peeples
Edited by Cindy Kenney
Printed in the United States of America

Elves Can't DUNK

Robert Skead

TaleBlazer PRODUCTIONS LLC

Dedication

For my family, who individually and as a whole, make my life wonderful! May the love of the Founder of Christmas reign in your hearts all year long!

Robert Skead

Contents

CHAPTER ONE

Jump Ball!

No one likes to be told they *can't* do something, especially when it's something you *really* want to do. Christmas elves are no different. Their *can-do* spirit helps them accomplish amazing things like balancing heavy wooden boxes on their noses and launching tickle fights while playing several instruments at one time. *That* is exactly what the elves were doing—tickling, singing, playing, and making toys at designated workstations. Each stroke of a paintbrush or bang of a hammer was matched perfectly in rhythm with the sound of music—Christmas music, of course. The song on the lips of each and every elf was a rockin' version of *Jingle Bells*. And as they sang it, they danced and grooved their little elf bodies to its jazzy beat.

It was a fun and wondrous sight—the dancing, singing, and toy making—only it was missing one thing—Sebastian!

Sebastian was nowhere to be seen or heard. You see, Sebastian is *not* your ordinary elf. Oh, he has pointed ears and is short like the other elves, but while everyone else at the North Pole was excited about Christmas, Sebastian had other interests—and the word *can't* just wasn't in his vocabulary—well, at least not on most days.

Sebastian was off to the side of the workshop looking through his telescope. "Yes! All right!" exclaimed Sebastian, as he threw his hands in the air joyfully. Then he quickly returned his eye to the telescope in front of him. Sebastian was wearing his official candy-cane striped overalls. Sebastian's smile widened as he peered through the viewfinder. Across the block, Santa was watching a basketball game on television, and with the help of a high-powered telescope, so was Sebastian! He laughed as he watched Santa dunk his chocolate chip cookie into hot chocolate at the same time an NBA player dunked the basketball into the hoop on TV.

Captivated by the game, Sebastian forgot all about his job of placing bows on top of presents. Meanwhile, present after present shot by him on a conveyer belt from a wrapping machine—each one waiting for him to place a bow on top. But that was *not* happening. Within just a few minutes, several hundred presents had piled up behind him.

"Wow, there he is," muttered Sebastian with awe as Frank Tanner, the coach of the Bears, appeared on the television screen.

Coach Tanner wore an expensive suit. His thick black hair was cut short. He angrily took off his tie and threw it at the referee after one of his players was called for a foul.

Sebastian zoomed in more closely on the game, unaware that Dudley, the head of the toy factory, was studying the whole scene and glaring at him. With every package that flew by Sebastian, Dudley's chubby face grew red as he huffed like an angry bull. Dudley ducked to evade a present that flew toward him causing his belly to jiggle up and down. The toy factory manager enjoyed too many of Mrs. Claus's homemade double chocolate donuts—and his jiggling belly was the result.

"Sebastian!" hollered Dudley. His voice boomed throughout the entire workshop and connected with the ears of each and every elf, and they immediately stopped singing and working. His bellow, however, startled Sebastian and caused him to jump back wide-eyed and land right on the conveyer belt. The speeding belt propelled Sebastian through the air like a bullet directly into Dudley, sending them both CRASHING into the pile of packages on the floor. As Sebastian stuck his head up through the mess, a large present awaiting a bow knocked the telescope over into the wall and broke it in two.

Dudley stumbled through the piles of boxes and made his way to his feet. "What do you think you're doing?" asked Dudley. He looked at all the elves staring at them, removed a remote control device from his pocket, and pressed a button. The entire assembly line came to a halt.

Sebastian looked up at Dudley with trembling lips.

"You've got the easiest job in the entire workshop!" Dudley shouted.

"Sorry, Dudley, sir," said Sebastian, cutting Dudley's sentence off. He watched as Dudley's face turned bright red making him look like a big apple with bulging eyes. Sebastian continued, "I, ah, was just . . ."

"Watching basketball!" Dudley finished Sebastian's comment. "I know! I don't want to hear it. All of these presents . . ." he started as he pushed his way through the packages scattered around him, ". . . are mixed up! Look how many don't have bows! Tags are on the floor. We don't know where they go now." Dudley was huffing and shaking his head. He searched for words and when he found them he addressed his staff. "Thanks to Sebastian here, you're *all* going to have to check every single one of these presents and make sure *nothing* is broken! And then, I want them *all* re-wrapped and tagged—and bowed! That means everyone is working overtime!"

Sebastian glanced at the hundreds of scowling elf faces throughout the workshop. "I'm sorry," he stated softly.

Dudley turned to Sebastian. "You're always sorry. Elves can . . ." Dudley paused and stopped himself from adding the T sound. "I mean elves *don't* play basketball. We make toys, music and cookies. We do lots of other things . . . all related to Christmas. Listen, Sebastian, since you're not being a good team player, maybe you should sit this one out. Your friends will pick up your slack." Dudley wiped off his trousers and stormed out of the workshop.

Angry silence filled the room, until . . .

"Gee. Thanks for the extra work Sebastian," cried several elves in unison.

"He didn't mean to give us more work, you guys." It was a cute young elf with strawberry-blonde hair named Holly. She was the only voice on his side. She was an apprentice in the Security Department and she hated to see her friend Sebastian in trouble.

Sebastian looked at Holly as if to say 'thank you.' Then his head fell low. He walked dejectedly out of the room. "Nobody cares about me around here," Sebastian said to himself. "But Santa loves hoops. He'd understand." Sebastian paused. "They'll see. I'm going to play in the NBA someday, and they'll all wish they were my friends."

CHAPTER TWO

No Time for Bowing

The stars above Santa's workshop twinkled brilliantly with an extra glow. It was as if they knew that Christmas was only a few days away and even they were extra excited for its arrival.

Sebastian treaded down the pathway that led to his room. He knew the beauty of a wintry night, and not even his saddened feelings could keep his head down for long. He slowly gazed upward and examined the sky. His heart jumped as he spotted a shooting star soar in the east. Toward the west, he gazed at the Northern Lights dancing in the air above.

Sebastian spotted a long pole with a sign on top that read:

NORTH POLE—THE TOP OF THE WORLD

He bent down, picked up some snow, and molded it into a ball. Then he took aim, wound up, and threw the snowball. It sailed through the cold air and collided with the sign, splashing it with snow. Sebastian wondered if he'd be a good baseball pitcher, but the thought only lasted a second—he knew his favorite sport would always be the one that involved dribbling and shooting.

Moments later, Sebastian arrived at the elves' quarters. With nothing to do and no one to talk to, Sebastian tucked himself into bed. It had been a very long day. Seconds later, he was asleep and snoring. Unlike the other elves who only dreamed about Christmas, Sebastian's mind took him to his place of dream-like bliss—an NBA arena!

Spotlights flashed all around the hardwood floor.

"And now . . . the point guard, at two-feet eleven, from Blizzard State . . . Sebastian!" the announcer's voice roared.

The crowd went wild and chanted, "Sebastian! Sebastian! Sebastian!"

Sebastian happily jogged onto the basketball court and ran through what seemed like a forest of knees as he high-fived his teammates who reached out their hands to slap his. The smile on his face measured ear to ear. The crowd continued to chant his name. It was Sebastian's favorite dream and one he just had to make come true.

* * *

The next day the North Pole was beautiful. A light snowfall during the night covered the entire workshop in a white blanket. Sebastian awoke with a start. Elves are notorious for their pointy ears, cute little laughs, and their loud snoring. They snored so loud that their blankets rose up in the air each time they exhaled. Sebastian covered his ears and jogged up to his closet. He took out his basketball, jersey, and sneakers and got dressed. He started to exit the door when he had an idea. He broke into a huge grin and started to dribble softly.

Bounce. Bounce. Bounce.

Not a single elf woke up.

Sebastian dribbled faster.

Bounce—bounce—bounce—bounce.

Sebastian continued to dribble faster and faster and faster!

BOUNCE—BOUNCE—BOUNCE!

His eyebrows rose in amazement. His roommates had not budged. Each comfortable snore seemed to bring them more and more pleasure and send them deeper and deeper in sleep. Sebastian spun the ball on his finger as if to congratulate his knocked-out roommates. Then he headed out the door.

By the time Sebastian arrived at the lake, the Polar Bear Club was in high gear. Some bears dove into the water from a cliff. Others swam while several of them sat on the bank wearing robes that bore the name of their club. The rest of the members of the Polar Bear Club were playing basketball. Today was their big game against the Walrus Warriors, a team made up of, you guessed it—walruses.

"Yo! Sebastian!" It was Ralphy, Sebastian's best friend who also happened to be a big, furry, white Polar Bear. Ralph's friendly face broke into a smile as he approached his friend in his basketball shorts and a jersey featuring his favorite number—00.

"Sorry I'm late. What's the score?" Sebastian yelled. He unzipped his warm-up suit revealing the same color jersey as Ralph's. Sebastian was Number 14.

"We're down ten to eight, so hurry up! Get in the game, buddy! Eleven wins!"

Sebastian quickly tied his high-top basketball shoes and

ran onto the homemade court. The backboards and hoops were constructed of fishing nets stuck into two opposite snow banks.

The game continued. The opposing team inbounded the ball and some seriously creative passing took place. The walruses handled the ball like the Harlem Globetrotters! They passed the ball behind their backs, from nose to nose, and from one player to the next as the bears struggled to keep up.

Sebastian, being much smaller and quicker than his walrus friends, intercepted a pass. He dribbled down court, evaded his defender, and took his favorite jump shot. It went up, up, up and IN!

The seals and penguins watching from the sideline applauded.

Ralphy ran up to Sebastian and gave him a low five. "Great shot!" he announced. "Two more points and we win!" They ran down court together.

Along one side of the court, a walrus was doing the play-by-play of the game. "Good morning everyone. This is Wally the walrus. We've got a score of Warriors 10, and Sebastian's Super Stars 9. Back on the court, Wilbur Walrus maneuvers the ball down toward the basket. He dribbles left, fakes right. Wilbur is one of the best players in the league this season. His team is the best the North Pole has ever seen! There goes Sebastian . . . he steals the ball! It looks like the skinny, little elf fouled him, but the referee doesn't call it. Oh! Come on Ref!

"Sebastian dribbles down court! He heads toward the basket . . . Whoa! Waldo Walrus dives headfirst for the ball, but he can't come up with it. Sebastian makes a quick move to get out of the way . . . and Waldo goes sliding like a bowling ball across the ice. He crashes into a bunch of penguins! Owww! Steeee-rike! There had to be a foul on that play, but no call again! Come on Ref!

"Sebastian dribbles up to Ralphy Bear who lifts him up for the dunk and they score again! I can't believe it!"

A penguin changed the scoreboard to read 10 - 10 and the game continued.

"The Warriors inbound the ball. Behind-the-back passes take the ball from one good-looking walrus to another. Wyatt Walrus is wide open! There's the pass . . . but Ralphy dives! Holy seal! He's sliding on his belly like a walrus! Of all the copy cat moves . . . I don't believe this! Ralphy slides . . . and he stops . . . and . . . yes, he intercepts the ball! Will someone blow the whistle out there?! That's gotta be an illegal move!

"Sebastian runs down court. He's wide open and Ralphy passes the ball. Sebastian puts his hands out for the catch . . . and . . . whoops! Yes, he dropped the ball! Waldo scoops it up, passes it to Wyatt, and they score! Yes! The Warriors WIN! The Warriors WIN!" the announcer shouted, then paused to catch his breath. "This is just as I predicted in our pre-game report. That, my friends, is one disappointed looking elf! He certainly blew this game," the announcer reported with a sarcastic tone in his voice. "Just a reminder, this morning's post game report will be brought to you by Sully's Snow Cones, the best tasting snow cones at the North Pole. This is Wally the walrus for NP Sports. We'll be back after these messages."

Everyone on the other team jumped up and down, celebrating their victory.

Meanwhile, Sebastian looked at his hands as if there were holes in them. He glanced at Ralphy who was shaking his head in frustration. Then a look of worry crossed Sebastian's face. He suddenly remembered he was supposed to be somewhere else, and he took off like a jack rabbit toward the workshop.

* * *

At the bowing station, Dudley sat on a stool tapping his shoe as he glanced at his watch. Sebastian came sliding through the door and skidded to a stop. As soon as he saw the look on Dudley's face, he knew he should never have gone to the basketball game.

"Sorry I'm a little late, sir," admitted Sebastian. "I lost track of time. But I'm here now. I promise I'll do an awesome job."

Dudley gave a Sebastian a look, then said, "No problem, Sebastian."

Sebastian couldn't believe his elfin ears. In fact, he stuck his index finger in his right ear to clean it out. "Who are you and what are you doing in Dudley's body?" Sebastian asked, trying to be playful.

"Oh, it's me all right," replied Dudley. "No time for bowing? Well, don't worry. You won't be bowing today or any day after this, Sebastian. I have a much better job for you."

"You do?" Sebastian smiled. Then he looked around excitedly at the toy factory and wondered what job it could be.

CHAPTER THREE
Dirty Jobs and Big Ideas

The air inside the stable was filled with the smell of hay. It was imported hay from Nebraska, a special gift from Santa for his team of eight reindeer. The stable also had other odors like the scent of Bayberry candles, which masked the fact that reindeer did not use bathrooms. This was a reality Sebastian knew firsthand because his new job was to clean out the stalls of Dasher, Dancer, Prancer, Vixen, Comet, Cupid, Donner, and Blitzen. It was a dirty job, but Sebastian figured he deserved it, not to mention that it was one job that maybe even he couldn't screw up.

For hours he used a pitchfork to scoop up old hay and replaced it with fresh hay. When it came time for a break, Sebastian stopped to relax for a moment. It was then that he spotted a pile of newspapers in the corner. He curiously walked over to them, picked one up off the top, and quickly found the sports section of the *Polarville Gazette*. The cover read:

FRANK TANNER AND THE POLARVILLE BEARS
TO PLAY CHRISTMAS DAY

It was dated yesterday. Sebastian's mind raced with excitement. If only he could try out for the Bears. Then he could leave the life of toy making, bowing, and cleaning stables and do something he really wanted to do. But how?

"Hi Sebastian!" It was Holly. Her kind voice rang out like music to Sebastian's ears.

"Oh. Hi Holly," replied Sebastian, as he quickly put the paper down and picked up his pitchfork. He couldn't believe that the one time he took a break all day was when she had chosen to come in. Even Dudley found him hard at work earlier in the afternoon when he had come in to check. There was an awkward pause as Sebastian tried to mask the fact that he liked Holly, maybe more than a friend. "Nice night, huh?" commented Sebastian.

"Yes, it is." Holly paused as she smelled the room. "It smells nice in here."

"Yeah, thanks to Mrs. Claus's homemade candles and me cleaning this place all day."

"Would you like to join me for some milk and cookies?"

Sebastian looked puzzled. "Aren't you still supposed to be at work?"

"Oh. We finished early so Dudley let us off."

"Really?" Sebastian was amazed. "Who put the bows on?"

"Oh that doesn't matter. How about those cookies? I bet they're right out of the oven like you like them."

"Who did the bowing Holly?"

"I hear Mrs. Claus made chocolate chip cookies and oatmeal cookies with raisons. I know you love raisins."

"Holly. Tell me."

Holly knew Sebastian wouldn't give up. "Well, if you must know. It was Wilson."

"That pee wee? Why he's the smallest elf in the entire North Pole."

"Seems his tiny fingers make him a super bower, but forget about that. Let's go get a treat. Mrs. Claus always has the milk at the perfect temperature."

Sebastian shook his head. "No. I wish I could, but I have to finish up in here."

"Ok then," said Holly politely. "I'll see you inside when you're done." Holly waved and left the stable. Sebastian noticed Donner had an itch and was rubbing his head against the latch on his stall. Sebastian strolled over and scratched behind his ear.

"You want to do some take-off practice?" asked Sebastian.

Donner's eyes widened with excitement.

Sebastian took him out of his stall and walked him over to the middle of the stable where a large, old treasure chest stood. Sebastian opened the chest. Inside was corn, but not any typical corn. It was special feed corn, the stuff that makes reindeer fly. It sparkled and twinkled like beautiful, tiny, yellow Christmas tree lights. "Here you go, pal. This will get you going," remarked Sebastian, as he grabbed a handful of corn and fed it to him.

Donner ate it and shook his head. Something magical seemed to happen to him. His fur vibrated. His heart raced like an engine. Then Donner began prancing right out of the stable until . . .

ZOOM!

Donner took off into the air!

Sebastian's mouth fell open a bit. "No matter how many times I see that, it is still *so* cool," he said to himself as some of the sparkling corn that had spilled on the ground caught his attention. He bent down to pick it up and stared at it.

Then it hit him—a big idea! Sebastian's head darted at the newspaper and his eyes locked on the picture of Frank Tanner. "What if I had some of this stuff at a tryout? I'd be a dunking *machine*." Sebastian wondered what it would feel like to soar through the air and dunk like an NBA star. As he pictured himself dunking baskets in his mind, his smile grew wider and the glow of the corn sparkled off his front teeth.

CHAPTER FOUR
Traveling

Later that night, when all the elves were asleep, Sebastian took out his duffel bag and packed his belongings. He stuffed his toothbrush, toothpaste, basketball shorts, sweat suit, shirts, and high-tops into his bag. Then he took out his special stash of snacks that he kept hidden away for when he had "the munchies." He put in some trail mix, cereal bars, apples and a few bottles of sparkling North Pole spring water.

With enough food to feed him for a day, Sebastian opened a cigar box that held all his special treasures. He took out an old Frank Tanner basketball card from his rookie year. The image on the front of the card showed Frank dunking a basketball. It made Sebastian smile. *Tanner, you are the coolest*, Sebastian thought. *I can't wait to be part of your team!* Sebastian placed the card, encased in a plastic holder, carefully into his pocket.

As Sebastian looked up, he fixed his gaze on the Santa figure smiling at him from atop his dresser. For his entire life Santa had been a constant example of what love and the Christmas spirit should be like in a person. Santa was kind and encouraging, and Sebastian knew that he would miss Santa most of all, but he knew they'd see each other again soon enough. Sebastian leaned his face in close to the figurine and flicked Santa's belly with his finger. It jiggled. "Bobble belly," Sebastian giggled.

Sebastian tiptoed across the room and looked back at his friends. *I'm gonna miss you guys,* he thought sadly to himself as he sighed and quietly closed the door behind him, ready for his new adventure.

* * *

As he quietly walked through Santa's Village, Sebastian looked up at the dark night sky. A speeding polar bear came sliding down a hill on his stomach and whizzed by, causing Sebastian to spin like a top. He twirled 'round and 'round until slowly coming to a stop.

"Hey Sebastian! What are you doing out here in the middle of the night? You want to go belly sleighing with me?" It was Ralphy. As always, he was happy to see Sebastian.

"No thanks," answered Sebastian as the world stopped spinning around him. "I always end up with snow down my pants."

Ralphy, stunned by his buddy's response, stopped dead in his tracks. His fur stood up at attention. "Are you kidding? You invented the quadruple belly whopper flopper! You're the master of disaster when it comes to tackling the snowy hills of the Pole."

Sebastian couldn't even look Ralphy in the eye. "That's just it. I *am* a disaster. Every time I try to do something, it becomes a catastrophe." Sebastian picked up some snow and formed a perfect snowball. He threw it at a nearby snowman and knocked the snowman's head off its body. The snowman's head rolled down the hill. It grew larger and larger with every rotation and smashed into a pile of firewood. Sebastian winced as he watched the impact and groaned, "See. I told you."

Ralphy placed his hand on Sebastian's shoulder. "Yeah, well . . . nobody's perfect. Look at me! I have a hairy back, but you don't see it getting me down, do ya? Come on, buddy! Let's belly slide!"

"Thanks Ralphy, but I want to do something big."

"Big, huh? That could be a problem. You're an elf, remember?" Ralphy smiled. But when he didn't get a reaction, he added, "Hey Sebastian, you may be small in size, but you've got a big heart, and I'm glad to be your big, furry friend." Ralphy gave his friend a great big bear hug.

"Thanks. You *are* my big furry friend," came the sound of Sebastian's muffled voice from deep inside a furry huddle. "Ralphy, please! Enough of the bear hug. I can't breathe!"

"Oh, sure. Sorry," Ralphy said, releasing him.

"I'm leaving," confessed Sebastian. "I'm going to try out for the Bears."

"The professional basketball team?"

"Yep." Sebastian grinned. "Hey, you should come with me."

"I don't think so."

"You can be my agent."

"You think you can get a tryout?"

"When Tanner sees me play, he'll freak."

"You'd be the tiniest player in the league," said Ralphy.

"The last time I checked, you seemed to have a . . . well . . . how can I say this nicely? Ahh . . . I can't. The truth is that you can't jump. You've got *no* hang time, which means *no* dunking. And buddy, *everyone* dunks in the NBA. You're kazoodles! I think maybe you've placed too many bows on too many presents."

Sebastian burst into a smile. "Oh, I can dunk . . . with a little help."

"I am *not* going to pick you up and hold you up to the basket so you can dunk at an NBA tryout," replied Ralphy, shaking his head and hand emphatically.

"You won't have to," replied Sebastian. "I can do much better than that. Follow me." Sebastian led Ralphy to the entrance of the stable and opened the door. The flickering light of a lantern inside barely illuminated the room where the reindeer slept peacefully. Sebastian walked up to the treasure chest, knelt down, and slowly opened the lid. Its contents sparkled. Sebastian reached in, grabbed a handful of the glistening corn, and showed it to Ralphy.

"Are you allowed to take that?" Ralphy asked.

"Well, I'm just taking a little. There's *plenty* here." Sebastian's eyes twinkled.

"But that's not yours. It's stealing," said Ralphy.

"It's just a little. No one will even know it's gone." Sebastian looked at the corn in his hand and felt guilty for a moment. He knew that professional basketball players are really tall and the sparkly magical corn would give him more hang time than Michael Jordan on the moon. He opened his duffel bag, scooped up some corn, and placed it inside. "Well, are you with me?" Sebastian's eyes told Ralphy that he really wanted him to come along.

Ralphy shook his head and sighed. "Oh man . . . I don't

believe I'm saying this, but . . . all right. Somebody has to watch out for you."

Sebastian gave Ralphy a high five. He closed the lid to the treasure chest and they left the stable. The night air was cold and it gave Sebastian a chill. He zipped up his jacket and climbed onto Ralphy's back. The two adventurers belly slid into the horizon towards Polarville.

CHAPTER FIVE
For the Love of the Game

The road to Polarville was covered with snow and within a few hours they were only a few miles from their destination. They found shelter in a cave and slept there until morning. Sebastian did not sleep much. Ralphy's growly snores were a much different sound and rhythm than the familiar elfin snores at home. Add all his thoughts about meeting Coach Tanner and the tryout swirling like a snowstorm in his head, and it was going to be a long night. But Sebastian didn't care. Today was going to be the best day of his life. When the sun rose, they got up, ate some of the food Sebastian packed, brushed their teeth, and headed for town. As they walked together, Sebastian felt more and more anxious. It was as if his dream was closer and closer to becoming real with every step.

The city of Polarville bustled with its usual morning activity. Cars, trucks, and buses whizzed by as Sebastian and Ralphy walked down the sidewalk toward the arena.

They were greeted by strange glances as people briskly strolled by.

"I don't like cities," Ralphy commented. "Let's go home."

"No way. Not yet," Sebastian said as he and Ralphy turned the corner. "Look! There it is!"

The building before them was huge and larger than anything at the North Pole. The name on the front of the structure read:

BOTTOMS UP DIAPER RASH
OINTMENT ARENA

The name was the result of recent marketing efforts that renamed almost every arena in the league. The facility held thousands of fans and was the home court of the Bears' professional basketball team. Thanks to the new arena's name, the Polarville Bears were known as the team that diaper rash built.

"Just think. He's actually in there somewhere . . . Slammin' Frank Tanner . . . my all-time favorite player! Of course, now he's the coach." Sebastian took the Frank Tanner basketball card out of his pocket. "When he played, he could do things with a basketball that would curl your fur. Hey, when I make the team, I'll see that you get a ticket to every game. They might even name a sneaker after me. What do you think about the name Air Sebastian?" Sebastian placed the card carefully back into his jacket pocket, quickened his pace, and headed for the Player's Gate entrance.

"I think something like that may have already been taken," Ralphy mumbled as he followed his friend toward the arena.

Inside, the Bears were practicing their drills. The men ran up and down the court wearing their practice jerseys and shorts. Although professional, the team was not very good. The team's best players were all injured. And the replacement players missed easy lay-ups, fumbled their dribbles, and sometimes even tripped over their own feet.

"No! No! Set your pick! This is basketball, not a clown convention! You guys dribbled better when you were babies!" Coach Frank Tanner screamed in his usual cranky manner. The six foot seven inch Tanner was wearing a blue sweat suit with his team's logo on it.

John Campbell, the owner of the team, watched the hijinks with disgust from the stands. "Hey Coach! Know what I want for Christmas?" the balding, gray-haired man yelled. "Fans in the stands again! Listen, we've got the Christmas Day game against the All Stars here in two days. You better shape this team up quick or you'll be coaching kickball at the local YMCA. Start winning or you're out of here!" Campbell's voice echoed throughout the arena as he limped from the stands to the corridor.

Coach Frank Tanner's head shot as it appears on the Polarville Bears' website. The coach only loves winning more than his special gold whistle.

Coach Tanner looked down at the floor in disappointment. He couldn't bear to watch his team play or even try to play anymore. Campbell's words struck a nerve in him that hurt. "Or you'll be coaching kickball," Tanner mimicked his boss. He turned to his assistant, Jenkins, who wore an old, brown suit. Jenkins was a plump little man with a face like a hog who would rather wallow in money than mud. His red hair was greased back and parted down the middle. "How many fan letters have I gotten recently?" Tanner asked.

"Fan letters? Jenkins paused and waved his hand. "Oh Coach, don't worry about fan letters. They're way over-valued and hardly a determination of popularity."

"How many?"

"One."

"But that was from our team doctor." Coach Tanner shook his head unhappily.

"He made lots of money on all our injuries." Jenkins tried to change the subject. "He sent us a Christmas card too."

Coach Tanner turned his attention to his players on the court. "You know what I want for Christmas, Jenkins?"

"A cheese grater?" Jenkins replied seriously.

"No, you dingbat!" Tanner hit Jenkins with a sport towel. Jenkins fell back, slipped, and landed on the floor.

Tanner shook his head. "What I *want* is a team of dunking, dominating, skyscrapers. Not these dimwits." He paused. "We *have* to end this losing streak. If these new recruits could jump higher and dominate the competition, then maybe we could actually win a game. They're not getting rebounds. Their shots are getting blocked. There's only so much I can do. I *hate* losing." Tanner looked down at his players sitting on the bench. Some wore knee braces and a few of them neck braces. "This team is killing my reputation," he said softly to himself.

On the court, a player maneuvered the ball past his

teammate. He then tripped over his shoelaces and knocked over four of his fellow players.

Coach Tanner winced. "Oh man, Jonesy! Have you been tying your own shoes again? Keating! I thought I told you to tie his shoes! And follow your shot next time!" Tanner looked at the ground and shook his head. "God, help us," he said to himself.

Just then, Sebastian and Ralphy anxiously entered the arena. Sebastian surveyed the practice in action. His eyes widened with excitement as he spotted his hero. "Wow," Sebastian said in awe. "There's Slammin' Frank Tanner, the king of the Super Duper Dunk. Come on." Sebastian grabbed Ralphy by the fur and they walked down the aisle to the floor of the court. Sebastian started walking confidently towards Tanner before Ralphy could utter a word.

"Come on ladies! The ball is supposed to go *through* the hoop!" Tanner clapped. "Let's go people!"

"Excuse me, Coach Tanner."

Tanner turned around, but saw no one. He paused, then looked down and gazed at Sebastian glaring up at him. Tanner closed his eyes to make sure he wasn't dreaming.

"Hi. I'm Sebastian. It's a tremendous pleasure to meet you, sir."

Tanner opened his eyes. The strange image before him had not changed. "Tryouts for mascots were held four months ago, kid. You're too late."

"Mascot? No, you don't understand. I'm here to see you," Sebastian paused and swallowed hard, ". . . and try out for the team."

Coach Tanner started to laugh. "What? You got to be kidding me!" Tanner noticed Ralphy and looked him up and down. "Nice costume. But the same goes for you . . .

tryouts for mascots were months ago. Aren't you hot in that thing?"

Sebastian and Ralphy exchanged innocent looks and shrugged.

"Excuse me, Coach. I'm not here for mascot tryouts. I want to play basketball." Sebastian declared.

Tanner's eyes widened with surprise. "I don't think that's gonna happen."

"Please Coach . . . I'm your biggest fan. When you scored sixty points against Chicago, that was awesome. I know everything about you! Frank Tanner, king of the Super Duper Dunk, first round draft pick for Portland, Rookie of the Year, and you led the league in scoring, rebounding, and assists five consecutive years."

As Sebastian talked, the look on Tanner's face began to change. His typical frown actually started to curl upwards into a slight, but ever-so-noticeable, smile.

Sebastian continued, "Blocked shots for four consecutive years. You always put your left sock on first. And your favorite ice cream is double chocolate fudge."

Tanner's mouth opened so wide that his chin practically hit the floor. "How'd you know that?"

"Like I said . . . I know everything about you."

"He does," Ralphy nodded in agreement.

Meanwhile, on the court, the players stopped playing and were staring at them.

Coach Tanner noticed and blew his whistle. The sound of the metal whistle was deafening. Tanner used every ounce of breath he had to belt out, "Back to work you knuckleheads! Let's go!" Then he turned back to Sebastian. "This is a man's game, kid. Come back and tryout when you're older and bigger. I've got work to do here. Thanks for the visit." Focusing his attention back on his team he barked, "Get back to your drills!" then walked away.

Sebastian stood motionless.

"Come on. Let's get out of here," Ralphy said as he took Sebastian by the arm and gently led him away.

Jenkins jogged up to Tanner. "Wait a second, Coach. Why don't you let him try out?"

Tanner looked at Jenkins as if he were from another planet. "Are you whacky?"

Jenkins leaned in closer to Tanner. "Look at him," he whispered. "Everyone's been so tense lately. We could use a good laugh. Let him try out. It'll be good for morale. Happy players *may* play better."

Tanner pondered the thought. A small smile appeared on his face, and he shook his head in agreement. "Hey, little rookie! Come on back over here!"

CHAPTER SIX
This Elf is Airborne!

Sebastian quickly turned around and ran back toward Coach Tanner.

"All right big guy, you've got five minutes to dazzle me," Tanner said convincingly.

"All right!" Sebastian put up his hand to Tanner for a high five, but Tanner didn't move a muscle. Sebastian smiled anyway and jogged up to Ralphy who was holding his duffel bag. Sebastian reached inside the duffel bag. He took out a small handful of corn, took a deep breath, and ate it.

"Let's go! Hustle! Hustle! Hustle!" Tanner called while clapping.

Sebastian ran out onto the court.

Tanner picked up a basketball and addressed his team. "Okay men. This is . . ." Tanner looked down at the little elf.

"Sebastian," said Sebastian as he shuffled his feet with excitement.

"He's going to try out for the team." Tanner held back his own laugh.

The team looked at him like he was crazy. "You got to be kidding us Coach," the players grumbled.

Tanner handed Sebastian the ball. "All right, kid," he chuckled. "Show us what you got."

Sebastian took the ball. His heart pounded. His eyes filled with determination. His dream was about to come true. This was his moment!

Tanner walked back to the sideline and joined his assistant.

"This should be great," said Jenkins.

Tanner looked towards the court. Sebastian already had the ball in play. His size and speed immediately worked in his favor. He easily maneuvered around the defense, leaving those trying to guard him dumbfounded. Then he took his favorite jump shot from three-point range. It went up . . . up . . . up . . . and IN!

Sebastian beamed. He looked at the empty seats around him and imagined them filled with fans screaming his name. Meanwhile, Tanner and everyone else in the gym stood there with their mouths wide open, shocked and amazed.

Next, the opposing team put the ball in play. A very tall player dribbled it down court until Sebastian stole the ball away and scored again with a jump shot from the top of the key. In fact, every time Sebastian touched the ball, he scored. He was having a great game and was very pleased with the way he was playing.

Sebastian dribbled down court and leaned into the player defending him. "Watch out, dude. I've got more moves than a naked Eskimo on ice."

The player laughed and Sebastian dribbled past him. He was once again open for the shot. It went up, up, up and IN!

SWISH!

"Nothing but net! Swwwwwish! That's my favorite sound in the world!" Sebastian said, as he ran down court like a seasoned pro.

Tanner and Jenkins nodded. They were confused, but impressed. As Sebastian scored again and again, they laughed in amazement. They couldn't believe that little Sebastian was playing so well, even against their team.

Sebastian dribbled down court for a breakaway play. There was nobody even close to him. *This is my chance*, thought Sebastian. *Time to dazzle the coach with a dunk.* Sebastian couldn't wait to experience the feeling of flying and dunking. His heart thumped in his chest. He took off and leapt into the air . . . but he barely left the ground. And he *missed* the shot!

"Elves can't dunk," said Ralphy shaking his head. "I knew it."

Tanner and the other players laughed.

"Okay, that's it!" Tanner yelled, having seen enough. "Practice is over!" He turned to Sebastian. "Sorry, kid.

We're just not interested. You've got a nice shot, but my grandmother has more hang time than you!" Tanner unzipped his warm-up jacket and headed for the water bottles beside the bench.

"Why don't you come back when you grow up," one player joked. "And I do mean *grow* . . . to about five feet!"

Everyone laughed.

Sebastian walked away with his head down low. *What happened? Why didn't it work? My dazzle went kerplazzle.*

Ralphy watched Sebastian for a moment, then picked up the duffel bag, and ran over to be by his friend's side. As they entered the hallway of the arena, the sound of laughter echoed behind them.

"What happened? Why didn't it work?" asked Sebastian.

"I have no idea," answered Ralphy. "That hero of yours sure is cranky."

Sebastian bent down and retied his shoes. "Oh, he's just having a bad day, and a bad season. The coach has a lot of responsibility and pressure. Coaching isn't easy, you know. Coach Tanner was a great player and he's a terrific coach. I just need to talk to him. I want a second chance." A determined Sebastian turned around and headed for the gym.

Ralphy followed. Even though Ralphy didn't agree with his friend's choice, he would always be there to support his friend.

The gym was now completely empty. Sebastian spotted a basketball on the floor and picked it up. "I don't understand what happened," admitted Sebastian. "The corn should have worked. I have to try again."

Meanwhile, a chipper Coach Tanner, feeling better thanks to having gotten a laugh, came back into the gymnasium too.

Sebastian looked at the basket before him. To someone of such short stature, the basket seemed like it was a mile high and to soar above its rim and dunk, almost impossible. Nonetheless, Sebastian dribbled down court. *One more try,* he thought. He approached the foul line and leapt into the air. Sebastian went up, up, up . . . soaring above the rim. He executed a perfect one-handed jam!

Tanner's mouth fell open. He stood frozen like a statue. When he realized his mouth was open, he quickly closed it, ducked down, and hid himself while licking his lips and drooling like a puppy.

"Yes! Did you see that?" Sebastian exclaimed. "This elf is airborne, Ralphy!" Then he paused and scratched his head. "I wonder why it didn't work before."

"You're not a reindeer. Maybe it has a delayed effect on elves," commented Ralphy.

"That felt incredible!"

"Well, you had a little help," Ralphy said as he held open the bag. The feed corn sparkled magically.

Tanner's eyes locked on the corn. He looked like he was about to explode. His eyebrows rose as he got an idea. His legs began to move up and down with anxiousness. He looked like he had to go to the bathroom really bad, but that wasn't what was on his mind. He snuck out of the gym and ran down the hall, jumping with joy every step or two. "Jenkins! Jenkins!" He ran up the escalator and down the hall. "Jenkins!" His voice bellowed through the arena until he got to his assistant's office. "Jenkins!"

"What?" Jenkins asked curiously, sitting behind his desk.

"Christmas just came early!" Tanner announced with joy. "That kid . . . that elf . . . holds the key to our future!"

"The . . . ah, elf? Ummm . . . Coach, maybe it's time you took that vacation?"

"I don't need a vacation!" snapped Tanner. "Oh, baby! Think of the possibilities." Tanner envisioned himself feeding the corn to his players. Immediately they turned into dunking machines. They ran and jumped and scored with amazing hang time! Even the shortest player on the Bears soared into the air and dunked the ball with ease. Then he saw himself on the cover of sports magazines as "Coach of the Year." He envisioned a scoreboard turning with wins and money falling down like rain all around him.

"I want that elf!" he yelled as he came out of his trance-like state.

* * *

On the basketball court, Ralphy watched Sebastian demonstrate his awesome, new dunking skills. Sebastian did every dunk his imagination could create—one-handed dunks, two-handed dunks, spinning dunks, somersaulting dunks. Sebastian was a sight to behold.

Tanner and Jenkins stepped onto the court. Their eyes widened as they watched tiny Sebastian perform his last somersault dunk. "Hello friends," Tanner said, briskly walking up to Sebastian and Ralphy.

"Hey new pals," followed Jenkins, with a hint of sincerity.

Coach Tanner looked at Sebastian's duffel bag. "That bag—may I see it?" His hand struck like a snake and grabbed it.

"Hey! That's mine!"

"Give it back!" Ralphy demanded, as he snatched a corner of the bag.

Tanner tugged on it hard. "Not yet."

"Coach, what are you doing?" Sebastian asked innocently.

"Yeah, you're not acting very nice," Ralphy said, pointing his finger at Tanner.

"Nice? There are moments for nice, but this isn't one of them!" Tanner cut them off with his overpowering voice and opened the bag. The corn sparkled inside. "Well, I'll be! Ho, ho, ho! Merry Christmas to *me*!"

"I don't like this." Ralphy looked at Sebastian with concerned eyes.

"Okay, my little friend. You're an elf. I get it, in fact, I love it," Tanner chuckled, giddily. Then, his tone changed. "This stuff . . . I know what it does. How long does it last?" Tanner asked as his eyes narrowed.

"One night," Sebastian answered. "Why?"

"One night, huh? Then there's not enough. Will this make *me* fly?" Tanner asked harshly.

"No. It only makes reindeer fly. It will make you jump *really* high though," Sebastian admitted.

Tanner laughed. "You know, I never believed in flying reindeer or even elves . . . until I saw you dunk that ball." He paused. "You, my little elf buddy, are going to take me to where there's more of this stuff. You see, I've got a player who's a lot taller than you, but he's still the smallest guy in the league. He could use some dunking help too. In fact, it would be awesome if all our players could jump higher. If you take me to where there's more of this stuff, I'll let *you* join my team."

"Deal," said Sebastian.

Ralphy's eyes widened with shock.

CHAPTER SEVEN
Naughty & Nasty Moves

By the time Coach Tanner, Jenkins, Sebastian, and Ralphy reached the North Pole it was nighttime. They quietly approached a hill that led to Santa's workshop. Tanner and Jenkins slowly climbed to the top and peeked over like spies on a secret mission.

"I can't believe you agreed to this. I don't trust that guy," said Ralphy.

"It's just a little bit of feed corn," replied Sebastian.

"It's not right. And it's cheating," Ralphy whispered.

"Shhh! Please be quiet down there!" Tanner said feeling a little edgy. He had never stolen anything before and it made him feel *different!* He was suddenly worried about getting caught and ruining his image. But he was also thinking about all those *wins!* The thought of that propelled him forward. "C'mon elfy. Let's hurry it up and get this over with."

"You better listen to the coach," sneered Jenkins, "or you won't get much play time when you join the team."

Join the team? The thought of that little elf on his team

made Tanner feel silly. He would be the laughing stock of basketball! He suddenly realized he wouldn't be able to follow through on his promise. Stealing and breaking a promise to his greatest fan—it was almost too much for Tanner to deal with. So he shrugged those thoughts aside and focused on the game—winning the game—coach of the year—awards—money—fame!

"Eh, coach?" Jenkins asked quietly. "Just how much playtime are you thinking of giving that elf?"

The question snapped Tanner back to reality. "None, you idiot. Once we have the corn, we won't need the little critter."

"Right! Of course not. Good play, coach." Jenkins snickered.

Jenkins excels at counting money. And yes, his underwear is even green with dollar signs. Too much information, we know.

Tanner scowled at Jenkins. He waved for Ralphy and Sebastian to join them at the top of the small hill. Then they all forged ahead down the hill into Santa's Village and quietly walked toward the stable.

"Coach, when my friends see me play for you . . . wearing that Bears' jersey, they're going to be *so* impressed. I'm not so popular with them right now," admitted Sebastian.

Tanner gazed down upon the tiny elf and nodded. "I know how you feel kid," Tanner said—and he did. He could still remember what it felt like to be unpopular when he was a kid. He really didn't want to hurt the little elf. He seemed like an okay guy, and there was no denying how much he adored Tanner. Still, this was the only way Tanner could think of to solve his overwhelming problems. Tanner felt like he'd hit a brick wall with no way of getting around it until he saw that magic corn. His best players were all hurt and those left seemed to get pathetically worse each day instead of better. The pressure to win more games was immense. If Tanner didn't turn things around fast, he would lose his job, his popularity, and everything he valued! This just had to work. Tanner looked at the buildings before him. "Now, show me where the stuff is."

"When I'm on your team, can I be your starting point guard?" asked Sebastian.

"Yeah . . . yeah . . . sure. Whatever you want. Just get me that sparkly stuff."

"We're almost there, Coach. After all, a deal is deal," Sebastian said looking up to his favorite all-time player. "Don't you worry, we'll snatch some corn, put it in my extra duffel bag, and we'll be out of here. No one will miss it."

"Oh yeah, about that . . ." Tanner said still visualizing the cheering crowds, reporters taking his picture and begging for interviews, a flood of new contracts coming in . . .

"About what, Coach?" Sebastian asked.

"About what?" Tanner asked, shaking himself out it. "Looks like I'm going to want *all* of Santa's sparkly to make my team awesome."

"*All* of it?" Sebastian gulped.

"Yes. All of it."

Sebastian locked eyes with Ralphy and whispered, "You were right. I think I made a mistake. I blew it again."

"Come on, stop whispering," ordered Tanner.

"Elves like to whisper," said Sebastian.

"Well, coaches hate it," said Tanner.

"Yeah, whispering sucks," added Jenkins. "Ain't that right coach?"

Tanner picked up a block of snow and smashed it on Jenkins' head. He was feeling edgy again. He didn't like having to go through with this plan, but he was more determined than ever. He just wanted to get it over with.

Meanwhile, Sebastian stole a glance at the stable. A look of concern washed over his face. Then he looked at the workshop. "Okay, Coach. The corn's inside, over there," he said, pointing to the workshop door.

Tanner's smile grew wider.

Meanwhile, Holly peeked into the elves' quarters looking for Sebastian. She hadn't seen him all day and was worried. The snoring sounds coming from her elf friends practically knocked her hat off. She covered her ears and closed the door.

Inside the workshop, Tanner, Jenkins, Ralphy, and Sebastian walked directly in front of a sign that read:

TOP SECRET
OFF LIMITS!
ELF SECURITY CLEARANCE A

"It's in there," said Sebastian.

"Really?" questioned Coach Tanner suspiciously.

"If you had stuff that could make reindeer fly, wouldn't you'd lock it up in a safe, Top Secret place?" asked Sebastian. "You wouldn't just leave it lying around in a stable somewhere," Sebastian added, mustering all the conviction he had. "Let me go first," he said, gently pushing Jenkins out of the way.

"No. Wait," instructed Coach Tanner. His face revealed a questioning look, as if he was still struggling with whether he wanted to continue what he'd started. Sebastian took another strategic step further. The coach noticed and said, "Nice try, little elf, but I don't like the way you're acting. Jenkins, *you* go first."

Jenkins jumped up and down with excitement like he was doing a jig. "Oh boy, this is great. We're breaking into Santa's Workshop! This is highly illegal. I love it! You know, Santa never gave me what I asked for when I was a kid."

"You must have been a naughty boy," said Sebastian.

Ralphy nodded. "Oh, he was a naughty boy all right."

"Yes, I was. And it's time I got even with Santa on behalf of all the naughty boys of the world," said Jenkins with a sneer.

Tanner smacked Jenkins with his hat. "Enough! Get in there, you dimwit."

Tanner walked closer to the door as Sebastian politely conceded to his request. This is just what he hoped they would do. Jenkins slithered up to the door, placed his hog-like face close to it, turned the doorknob slowly, and opened it. Since the doors were made for elves, Jenkins immediately hit his head on the frame. "Owwww!" exclaimed Jenkins as he entered.

"You're a nincompoop," declared Coach Tanner walking right behind him.

Suddenly, red lights flashed. Sebastian quickly pushed Ralphy out of the way as a mechanical arm came out and grabbed Tanner and Jenkins. It shook them furiously, like two bottles of salad dressing.

In the elves' room, a sign flashed:

INTRUDER ALERT

and an alarm sounded, but an elf cap that had been thrown over the speaker muffled the sound so it wasn't loud enough to wake anyone up above their snoring.

Back in the Top Secret room, the arm of the security device finished shaking Coach Tanner and Jenkins and placed them inside a cage designed by Spalding, the North Pole's genius inventor. Although he had planned for intruders to be larger than elves, he never planned for anyone to be as tall as Coach Tanner. His height and size prevented the door from closing securely.

Tanner and Jenkins sat inside all scrunched up like they were about to explode. They both saw imaginary stars swirling around their heads.

"Well, well, well . . . look what we have here," said Sebastian. "You two thought you were so smart. Breaking into Santa's Workshop . . . very naughty."

"As soon as I can focus and stop seeing ten of you, I'm getting out of this thing, and coming after you . . . you smart-aleck elf!" Tanner yelled in a disoriented voice. "I thought we had a deal!"

"We did—but you made it a bad deal, Coach," answered Sebastian. "But Santa will be anxious to meet you. He's a big fan, but I don't think he's going to like this one bit. I'm surprised he and other elves aren't here by now."

"Ah!" Tanner yelled in frustration. "You two be quiet or I'll gag you myself! All I've got to use are two sweaty and very smelly gym socks!"

"Make that four," sneered Jenkins. He held up his feet. The odor practically pulsated from them. Ralphy and Sebastian locked their lips shut. Then, Sebastian turned to Ralphy and noticed the door of the cage swing open. His eyes widened as Tanner and Jenkins popped out. They tried to get up but looked like toddlers just learning how to walk.

"Come on!" shouted Sebastian. He grabbed Ralphy by the fur of his arm and they ran to a section of the workshop filled with Super Drenching toy water guns. Sebastian stopped in his tracks, picked one up, and pulled the trigger. He smiled as high-pressured water came out of the gun's nozzle.

"Go get Santa and everyone else. I'll take care of Tanner."

Meanwhile, Tanner and Jenkins regained their balance and perspective.

"Being dizzy makes me thirsty. Do you think they have a soda machine around here?" Jenkins asked.

Tanner was just about to smack him with his hat when he noticed a shelf full of walkie-talkies. He ran over to it and picked up two units. "Here, take one of these. We'll split up. You go that way. I'll go this way. I didn't come all the way here for nothing. I want that elf . . . and the corn!"

While Ralphy trotted toward the elves' quarters, Sebastian crawled on his hands and knees so he would not be seen.

Jenkins was doing his best impersonation of a ballerina as he carefully tiptoed around the corner and stopped.

Sebastian slowly took aim at him with his water drencher. "Hasta la vista, baby." He pulled the trigger. Highly-pressurized water came streaming out of Sebastian's gun. He hit the "ON" button of the automatic assembly line, and Jenkins was swept up onto the line by the machine. His walkie-talkie dropped onto the floor as Jenkins was hammered, glued, painted, boxed, taped, and at the very end of the process—wrapped! The package came off the assembly line and fell gently onto the floor.

"Every present must have a bow," observed Sebastian as he picked up a bow and expertly placed it on top. "You'll be a nice present for some naughty boy or girl," Sebastian admitted with a laugh. Then he noticed the walkie-talkie on the floor and picked it up. He activated the unit. "Okay, Coach. Jenkins is a little . . . wrapped up right now. So it's just *me* and *you*, and I've got home court advantage."

Sebastian's words came over loud and clear through Tanner's walkie-talkie as he crept through the opposite end of the factory. He unclipped the walkie-talkie from his belt. "And everything at your home is so very colorful," said Tanner as he jogged back toward where he left Jenkins. He banged his head on a low overhang and screeched, "Owwww! Everything in this place is also extremely small. How irritating! Now, I'm annoyed. I hate losing! I'm tired of losing! Now it's my turn to win! I'm comin' after you and that corn!"

It was at that moment that Ralphy entered the elves' main bunkroom. "Wow! These elves snore louder than a million barking walruses," he snickered, then covered his ears as he gazed across the room. There was an endless sight of nightcaps and blankets rising and falling—rising and falling through the nighttime air, which almost made him laugh. Then, he remembered why he was there. "Wake up!" he bellowed at the top of his lungs.

The elves continued to snore. Ralphy sprang into action and turned their beds over, dumping elf after elf onto the floor, until they finally woke up.

"What's happening?" asked Dudley.

"Get into the workshop! We've got intruders!" answered Ralphy.

All the elves jumped up, put on their robes, and bolted out the door.

CHAPTER EIGHT
Hot Pursuit

While the elves were running toward the workshop like a herd of angry chipmunks, Sebastian was crawling around like a baby inside of it. He maneuvered to his right slowly, putting one elbow in front of the other, only now he was directly in Tanner's sight.

Like a cat after its prey, Tanner moved into action and crept up behind him. Then he sprang from his position and lunged after Sebastian's leg . . .

The workshop entrance door slid open and revealed *hundreds* of screaming elves! The piercing noise was deafening.

Tanner's heart skipped a beat.

Sebastian recoiled from Tanner's grip, quickly scrambled to his feet, and darted away.

Tanner slowly stood up, gasping in astonishment as he stared blankly at the elves.

"There he is! Let's get him!" an elf yelled, sounding tougher than a 350-pound NFL linebacker.

A look of worry crossed Tanner's face. *This is definitely*

not good, Tanner thought, and although his brain sent a message to his legs to run, they remained planted firmly in place. He looked down at his feet and then at the elves. They looked like a blur of mini cheetahs on two legs quickly descending on him. When his legs finally received the message from his brain, he took off towards the other end of the workshop as the elves gained on him.

Sebastian watched as Tanner scurried away like a rabbit being chased by wolves through the workshop and out the door. Anxious to catch him, Sebastian joined his pals in hot pursuit.

Tanner's extremely long legs kept him well in front of the elves, afraid of what they might do with him if he was caught. As he ran, the coach felt his gold whistle, which he never removed from his neck, bounce around inside his shirt. Tanner also noticed that his injured right knee that ended his career wasn't bothering him. He attributed this to the extremely cold weather and the adrenaline running through his veins.

Tanner was gaining some real headway until he hit the ice and snow-covered ground where he slipped and slid. On top of that, he was a bit out of shape so he grew tired much faster than back when he was in the game. Tanner needed to rest and that meant finding a place to hide. He quickly zigzagged around some trees, then ditched behind a fence for cover as the elves ran past him. After they were gone, Tanner spotted the stable and decided that would be the perfect place to catch his breath and hide.

He ran for the entrance and slowly opened the door. The dimly lit dwelling was quiet and peaceful. He scanned his surroundings for a hiding place. Then he spotted it—an over-sized treasure chest! "They'll never look for me in there!" Tanner chuckled to himself. Coach Tanner stopped in mid-motion as he opened the lid and lifted his leg to enter the chest. His mouth dropped open. "Merry Christmas to *me*!" he exclaimed as he drank in the sight of the sparkling feed corn. "There's enough of this magic sparkly stuff to win a hundred championships!" For the first time in years, Tanner was actually starting to like Christmas, but for all the wrong reasons.

While Tanner stood drooling over the feed corn, Ralphy burst into Santa's bedroom, and yelled, "Santa! Get up!"

Santa Claus popped up from his sleep and quickly tried to gain his senses. "Ralphy? What's the matter?"

"Two guys are trying to steal the feed corn!"

"Who?"

"Coach Tanner and his assistant, Jenkins," Ralphy said.

"All right. I know them," said Santa, now fully awake. "Coach Tanner was the king of the Super Duper Dunk. He was always pretty well behaved, but Jenkins was *not* a very good little boy. Let's go."

Santa jumped out of bed wearing an undershirt and boxers with candy canes on them. Ralphy looked away while Santa quickly got dressed. Seconds later, they bolted out the door.

Back in the stable, Tanner grunted as he dragged the heavy treasure chest toward Dasher who watched him fearfully. The other reindeer wanted to help their friend, but Tanner had locked the rest of them inside their stalls.

"Sebastian? Are you in here?" It was Holly.

Coach Tanner heard her voice and hastily slipped behind a door to hide.

"Sebastian . . . is that you? I've been looking for you all day," Holly said softly, hoping to hear her favorite elf's voice in return. "Sebastian . . . where are you?" Holly slowly crept inside the darkened stable. Something didn't feel quite right to her, but she wasn't sure what it was. Holly examined the room. Everything seemed all right, but as she turned to leave, Tanner popped out from behind the door and jumped out at her.

"Who are you?" she asked with her big bright eyes opened wide with fear.

Coach Tanner paused, then said, "Me? Well . . . I'm Sebastian's favorite basketball player," said Tanner with a smile. "Just here for a little visit. Do you know how to fly these reindeer?"

"Yes, of course," answered Holly.

Tanner was taken in by the polite young lady elf, but at the same time he was afraid of getting caught and furious with Sebastian.

"Good. Can you show me how it's done?" Tanner asked, trying not to frighten her. After he pulled Dasher out of his stall and dragged the chest of feed corn closer, he saw that it wasn't working.

"Where's Santa?" asked Holly, unaware of what was happening.

"Santa? I'm guessing he's asleep. But don't worry, he's one of my biggest fans! He's invited me here many times, but I just haven't had a chance to visit until now. He told me to make myself at home."

Holly looked at him suspiciously, not believing what he said. "It's not time for flying practice now. Maybe tomorrow or maybe you can join us on Christmas Eve? You'll be amazed at how fun it is here that night."

Tanner tensed. He knew his time was limited and he didn't have any more time to be polite. "Look, I've got a special mission and I need to get this reindeer up in the air. I don't have time to mess around. Please show me how it's done."

Holly slowly started to back up as she said, "I'm sorry. I just c-can't."

That was it. Tanner had used up every ounce of patience. "I'm not going to say this again. Show me how to ride this thing, or I'll rip Dasher's antlers off and make me a coat rack," sneered Tanner.

"You wouldn't do that," commented Holly. "That would hurt him!"

Tanner rolled his eyes. "Just show me how to fly this reindeer!"

In the village, Santa and Ralphy were running down the street and were met by Sebastian.

"Sebastian! Where is Tanner?" asked Santa hurriedly.

"I don't know. Do you want to ask him yourself?" said Sebastian.

"What do you mean?" questioned Santa.

Sebastian held up the walkie-talkie in his hand and said, "He's got the other one."

Santa took the walkie-talkie from Sebastian.

"Frank Tanner, come in please. This is Santa. Come in. Over."

Tanner heard the voice come from his walkie-talkie. He smiled. Never in his wildest dreams did he ever think he'd actually get to talk to the one and only Santa Claus. He took out his walkie-talkie and cleared his throat. "Eh-hem . . . hey there, Mr. Claus. I've enjoyed my tour of your workshop, but I'm afraid it's time for me to go."

"He's taking Dasher!" shouted Holly.

"Quiet!" snapped Tanner. He placed his index finger to his mouth and made a pleasant "Shhh" sound to Holly.

"He's got Holly!" Sebastian said as a look of anger appeared on his face. "We have to get back to the stables."

"Wait!" Santa held up his hand for Sebastian and Ralphy to stop and they immediately halted. Santa clicked his walkie-talkie. "Frank," said Santa, calling the coach by his first name. "Let's put an end to this. If you want the corn, I'll give you some. But I know you really don't want that, because it would be cheating. You're a good enough coach to win without cheating."

"I know I'm good enough, but a coach is only as good as his players. And mine need all the help they can get!"

"Okay, Dasher, go ahead and do whatever he says. You'll be all right. I know Frankie. Deep inside, he's a good boy," Santa spoke gently into his walkie-talkie. "Don't you worry, either, Holly. Frank won't hurt you."

"The one thing that I've learned is that 'Good Boys' finish last and boy am I tired of finishing last. Later, Santa!" Coach Tanner said. Then he carelessly fed Dasher some of the corn, spilling it onto the ground as he rushed to leave. He latched the lid of the treasure chest and dragged it on top of Dasher's back. "Let's go Dasher . . . and no funny business." The coach hoisted himself onto the reindeer's back, clutching the chest close to both of them. "Let's get going," he added, about to give Dasher a kick with his heel.

"If you take the corn, then Santa's reindeer won't be able to fly," said Holly with extreme concern. "Then there'll be *no* Christmas."

Tanner paused, then said, "Santa's smart. He'll figure something else out. Sorry kid, but this stuff is gonna bring me many championships and more fame than you can imagine."

"But think of all the children in the world who'll be disappointed Christmas morning if there are no presents under their tree." A tear welled up in Holly's eye.

The coach hesitated. He glanced at the trunk and then at Holly and the sparkling feed corn spilled on the ground. Once again he saw his team winning over and over as bag after bag of fan letters were delivered all around him. He ignored Holly, leaned into Dasher, and said, "Launch us. Now!"

"Hold on tight!" instructed Holly. "That's really important . . . that and balancing." Despite her anger and disappointment, Holly didn't want to see anyone get hurt.

The other reindeer in the stable looked at Dasher, wishing they could help.

Coach Tanner put his left hand onto Dasher's antler and held it like a handlebar on a bike. Dasher started to prance. Suddenly, Holly bolted into action and jumped onto Dasher's back, wrapping her arms around Coach Tanner's hips. Within seconds, they were out the door and in the air.

"What are you doing?" shouted the coach, looking back at Holly.

"Santa needs that corn!" declared Holly. "I'm going with you whether you like it or not!" As an apprentice in the Security Department, Holly knew she had to do something, and she wasn't going to let a thief get away easily. Holly looked down toward the ground and spotted Santa, Sebastian, and Ralphy running toward the stable just in time to see them take off.

"I'm going after him," declared Santa. He turned to Sebastian and Ralphy. "You stay here." Santa ran into the stable, took out Donner, and hitched him up to a small sleigh. Santa reached into his pocket and took out a small leather pouch. He poured some feed corn into his palm and fed it to Donner. Then he jumped into his sleigh, took hold of the reins, and whistled. Donner started to prance and seconds later he was airborne with the little sleigh zooming along behind him.

At that moment, all the other elves arrived. They saw Santa and Donner in the moon-lit sky and spotted the coach, Holly, and Dasher flying away in the distance.

"We *have* to do something," stated Ralphy, "but what?"

"Follow me," insisted Sebastian as he marched toward the stable.

Dudley rushed to catch up with him and said, "Sebastian, what's going on?"

CHAPTER NINE
For the Love of Corn

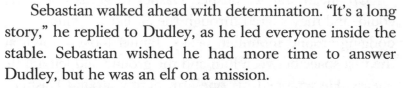

Sebastian walked ahead with determination. "It's a long story," he replied to Dudley, as he led everyone inside the stable. Sebastian wished he had more time to answer Dudley, but he was an elf on a mission.

"Look!" Ralphy shouted when he saw the spilled corn sparkling on the ground.

"That's great! We can use it to help Santa!" Sebastian picked up the feed corn and gazed at it in his hand. Then he unbolted two stall doors, took out Blitzen and Comet, and fed them some corn. "There's not a whole lot, but I hope it's enough," Sebastian confessed. "I'll take Blitzen," said Sebastian as he jumped on the reindeer's back.

Ralphy cautiously mounted Comet. "I don't have a license for this," he said nervously.

"Just hold on. They know what they're doing," Sebastian said.

"Be careful," Dudley warned.

"Take down that overgrown human," said Wilson. The tiniest elf managed to make his voice sound pretty tough.

"Bring him back and we'll show him not to mess with elves!"

Sebastian nodded his approval.

The reindeer started prancing, then . . .

ZOOM!

"Whoa!" yelled Ralphy, closing his eyes. He was a little scared and the very *first* polar bear in history to fly! If only his bear friends could see him now.

In the sky, Santa and Donner surveyed the horizon. "There they are!" shouted Santa, spotting Tanner, Dasher and Holly in the distance. Donner steered himself straight for them.

Up ahead, Tanner pushed Dasher to go as fast as he could, and they soared through the air like a fighter plane, dodging around mountain peaks. Tanner looked down at the vast space between him and the ground and felt a little queasy. He wrapped his one arm tightly around Dasher's neck as if holding on for dear life. In the other hand, his knuckles turned white grasping the leather strap that held the chest on Donner's side.

Holly kept her arms secured around Coach Tanner. Her mind raced for a solution. She had been telling Santa for months that they needed better security at the North Pole, and now she was living her worst nightmare. "Turn us around and return the corn immediately!" she shouted.

"Not happening," replied the coach.

Holly tried another approach. "If you turn around, I'll make you an extra special basketball. One that will never lose air or its bounciness. I'll even engrave your name on it."

"Nice try, cute little elf girl," said Tanner.

Holly rested her cheek against his back to block the

wind. "I don't know how my Sebastian could ever have you as his favorite player," she confided.

Coach Tanner did his best to block out her words as he too held tightly onto his flying reindeer and the chest of magic feed corn.

As they gathered speed, the air became colder and colder. Snow started to fall, making visibility and flying extremely difficult. Tanner wished he were flying first class in an airplane as he was accustomed to doing. His only comfort was the chest of corn that he held onto firmly with his one free hand. "Head for Polarville," Tanner instructed Dasher as his teeth began to chatter.

Santa took out the walkie-talkie and raised it to his mouth. "Frank. Come in, Frank. Please come back."

Dasher slowed down a bit so Tanner could gain better balance on his back.

Tanner pushed the button on his walkie-talkie and replied, "Sorry. I don't think so, Santa."

"Look Frank. I know it's been tough for you," Santa said with a sympathetic voice.

"What do *you* know about tough?" Tanner responded angrily. "Everything is nice and happy in your world . . . elves singing, cookies baking . . . you don't know anything about tough."

"Oh, but I do Frank. I know all about you—the bum knee that cut short your career, your team owner constantly reminding you about attendance records, and the press's relentless publication of your losses. You've really lost a lot of your love for the game—and your love for life."

Tanner didn't respond. He was speechless, almost in a

trance, and dumbfounded that Santa knew so much about him.

"I even know how much you miss your Mom, especially around Christmas time," Santa said, his voice gentle and sincere. "Don't lower yourself to this, Frank. Cheating won't make you feel any better—if anything, you'll feel much worse. There are other ways to win. Please consider this."

After a brief pause, the coach shook his head violently, bringing himself back to reality. "You don't get it, big guy. I'll feel plenty good after I win all those championships. And as for you—well—we don't always get what we want, now do we? You didn't seem to care about what I wanted when I was a kid."

Santa chuckled softly and said, "You wanted a million dollars and your own Learjet!"

"And I never got it. And you call yourself Santa Claus!"

Dasher looked at the coach, whose face was only inches from his own. He and Holly couldn't believe someone was actually talking to Santa Claus like this.

Tanner gave Dasher a hard stare, and Dasher immediately looked straight ahead again.

"Santa is a very wise man," said Holly. "You would be wise to listen to him."

Tanner had had enough of this conversation. "That's it. It's the fourth quarter with a minute to go, and I'm up by ten. Over and out!" He flipped the switch on his walkie-talkie and clipped it to his belt. Then he gave Dasher a harsh kick to make him fly faster and said, "Let's move! I'm gettin' cold!"

"You're never going to get away with this," scolded Holly.

Suddenly, a flock of snow geese appeared out of grouping of clouds, and they flew right **SMACK** into them! Geese were everywhere! One goose flew right into Tanner's chest and knocked him and the treasure chest completely off Dasher.

"Yaaaaoooowwwww!" Tanner bellowed through the cold night air.

A loud shriek followed as Holly teetered and slipped off too, but she managed to grab Dasher's leg. "Help!" she screamed as she dangled high above the ground holding onto her friend for dear life. She looked down and saw Tanner plummeting toward the ground like a ton of bricks.

Freezing cold air rushed by Tanner as he plunged . . . down, down, down . . . with the treasure chest held tightly in his hand. For an instant he felt sorry about copying his friend's homework in 6th grade, about walking past a cute little boy who wanted his autograph when he played basketball, and even about screaming at his team after they lost their games. Scene after scene flashed through his head, each one something bad he had done and now regretted. His life felt like a series of mistakes until . . .

THUMP!

Tanner hit the ground and rolled in the snow like an oversized snowball towards a cliff. His eyes bulged as he slid down a steep hill, and he frantically dug the fingers of his left hand into the snow to stop himself, but his effort was useless. Then the ground ended beneath him and he toppled over the cliff.

"Heeeeeelp!" Tanner shrieked.

As he fell to his demise, Tanner quickly reached out to grasp at a protruding branch and caught it! He hung from the tiny branch like a big wet drip preparing for its final plunge.

"Heeeey! Somebody help! Anyone?" Tanner's voice cracked. Tanner looked down at the treasure chest dangling at his side. There were jagged rocks directly beneath him, followed by a huge slope of snow that led to another cliff. Beyond that was a drop that measured thousands of feet.

Up above, Holly was still dangling from Dasher's leg, so he carefully eased up on his speed to try and help her. She tried with all her might to pull herself up, but just couldn't do it as snowflakes the size of baseballs fell all around them. Dasher looked below for a safe place to land. All he could see was jagged mountain tops and snow-covered rocks, so he kept flying slowly.

Thanks to the storm, Santa and Donner could not see more than fifty feet in front of them. Santa remembered his walkie-talkie and took it in hand. "Coach Frank. Come in. This is Santa. Where are you?" Santa paused to wait for his response. When the coach didn't answer, Santa and Donner sped up as much as they dared and kept looking.

Coach Tanner heard Santa's voice come out of his walkie-talkie. With one hand holding onto the branch for dear life and the other holding the treasure chest of magic feed corn, he did not know what to do. "I can let go of the branch and grab the walkie-talkie," he said to himself, "but then I'll plunge to my death. *Not* a good idea. I could let go of the magic feed corn and grab the walkie-talkie, but then I'd lose the corn and my chance to win all those championships. Nope, I don't want to do that either." Tanner weighed all his options carefully and refused to let go of the corn.

Meanwhile, in the sky above, Sebastian and Ralphy flew their reindeer like jet fighter pilots. "I don't see them anywhere! Do you?" shouted Sebastian.

"No!" replied Ralphy, wishing he were back home in his cozy bed instead of flying on a reindeer chasing an overgrown human.

Sebastian reached into his pocket and took out the basketball card revealing the image of Coach Tanner. *If only I hadn't taken the corn, then we'd never be in this situation,* he thought. Putting the card back away in his pocket, he continued to scan the horizon. He carefully searched for Santa or Coach Tanner until . . .

. . . suddenly Ralphy and Comet began to lose air speed and altitude. "Uh, Houston, we have a big problem," grunted Ralphy, looking extremely worried.

Sebastian turned around and saw his friends descending. "Oh no! There wasn't enough corn!" exclaimed Sebastian. He knew his reindeer couldn't handle the weight of two more passengers. That left only one conclusion as Sebastian would never leave a friend in need. "We'll have to go down!"

"I don't exactly think we have a choice!" Ralphy yelped as he and Comet slowly drifted down towards the ground.

Sebastian gazed through the falling snow. As he peered between the gigantic snowflakes, he suddenly saw something. "Look!" he shouted. They all focused on the area up ahead and spotted the familiar figure of a reindeer. "Head over there!" Sebastian instructed.

"Heeelp, somebody pleeeease!" yelled Holly.

"Hurry!" shouted Sebastian as Blitzen picked up speed. The wind carried Holly's voice and as they neared, Sebastian could see that Holly was not on top of Dasher where she belonged, but below him—and hanging onto his leg.

"Hurry Blitzen! Get up next to Dasher!" ordered Sebastian.

Blitzen surged forward, but a moment later, began losing his altitude as well.

Holly's fingers were getting tired and cold, and she was losing her strength. Dasher could feel her grip begin to loosen around his leg.

Sebastian leaned in and looked Blitzen in the eye. "Come on Blitzen buddy. Give it everything you've got."

Blitzen grimaced and pushed with all his might until they once again escalated and flew higher. They were closing in on Holly and Dasher again.

"Help!" screamed Holly. She looked up at her fingers and knew she could not hold on much longer. She said a silent prayer.

As Blitzen neared Dasher, Sebastian fought the wind and balanced himself on Blitzen's back.

"Be careful!" shouted Ralphy, watching the scene from below as he and his reindeer continued their gentle descent toward the ground.

Pushing with all his strength, Blitzen flew up right next to Dasher.

Then, like a cowboy switching horses during a ride, Sebastian leapt onto Dasher's back as a gust of wind crashed into him, knocking him away. Sebastian reached out and grabbed Dasher's neck, then spun himself around. Then, like a wrestler, he wrapped his legs around Dasher's torso and bent down to reach for Holly.

Just as Holly's hand lost her grip, their hands came together and united. Sebastian strained with all his might and pulled her up. For a brief moment, the two young elves met face to face and closed their eyes as if to kiss.

"Thanks for saving me," Holly whispered.

"You're welcome," Sebastian whispered back.

They were both interrupted by the sound of Ralphy's voice. "Hey buddy! Are you guys okay?" he bellowed.

Sebastian shook his head like a baby rattle as he came out of his trance. He looked down for his best friend and answered, "Yes! We're okay!"

"Ah, thanks for yelling in my ear," Holly said, doing her best to pull away from her new hero.

"Oh, sorry," Sebastian said, a little embarrassed and disappointed their moment was over. "Where's Coach Tanner?"

"I don't know. He fell off back there," answered Holly.

As they both turned their heads to look behind them, Dasher began to sink.

"Oh no! Here we go again!" shouted Sebastian. As they slowly floated downward, he noticed a small flash of light reflecting off something from below. "What was that? Did you see it?" he asked.

"I don't think so," Holly answered.

"Dasher, look! There's a safe place to land over there!" Sebastian yelled directing the reindeer towards the reflecting light.

A few hundred feet below, Coach Tanner's metal whistle caught a ray of moonlight causing it to briefly flicker brightly through the snowy night.

Tanner looked at his hand holding the branch and realized he couldn't hold on forever, so he decided to try and swing himself toward a nearby ledge. Back and forth he swung the treasure chest to the left and then the right, trying to move his body closer to safety. With each gentle swing, Tanner got closer to being able to launch his body onto the ledge until suddenly . . .

. . . the branch started to bend and snap.

He stopped and held his breath.

"That was *not* a good idea," he told himself as his mind searched for a new solution.

CHAPTER TEN
The Cliff Hanger

Dasher, Blitzen, Holly, and Sebastian landed near Ralphy and Comet. Thanks to the deep snow everyone made it down safely. Sebastian jumped off Dasher and ran toward the direction of the reflecting light. The reindeer, Holly, and Ralphy followed.

As Sebastian approached the area where he thought he'd seen the reflection, he looked around but saw nothing or no one. There was only a cliff. Then he heard a strange sound . . . like a grunt. Sebastian decided to investigate. Very carefully, he peered over the cliff's edge. His stomach clenched. He saw nothing, and yet he heard that same grunting sound again. He expected to see a bird or some other wintry animal, but never . . .

"Coach Tanner! What are you doing?" hollered Sebastian. "Hold on! We'll get you up!"

"Could you hustle it up please?" Tanner begged.

"Ralphy! Hurry!" Sebastian called.

Ralphy ran over to Sebastian, slowly peeked over the edge, and saw the coach. He stretched out his paw and reached down to grab him, but the branch began to break.

Tanner started to lose his grip. He was certain it was over.

Just as he started to fall, Ralphy lunged down and grabbed him. "Gotcha!" He looked down at the coach and saw the brief moment of fear disappear from Tanner's eyes. Then he noticed the jagged rocks. Ralphy had never saved anyone before and the act made him feel good inside. He secured his hind paws and tried to pull Tanner up, but both Tanner and the treasure chest were just too heavy to lift. Ralphy grunted and pulled. Beads of sweat fell from his furry face into the icy snow. "I . . . I . . . can't do it. How much do you weigh?" Ralphy asked in frustration.

"About 250," Tanner answered. "I've got a long frame to fill and it's getting longer! Would you please pull me up so I can get outta here you stupid bear!"

"Oh, so now you realize I'm no mascot," Ralphy replied as he struggled to move Tanner another inch closer. "If you'd let go of that chest of magic feed corn, I could pull you right up with no trouble."

"No way," Tanner answered, shaking his head. "I'm not gonna do it."

Ralphy started to lose his footing and now both he and Tanner started to slip. "Let go Tanner! If we fall, you aren't going to need that corn! There won't be any need for anything!" Ralphy groaned as they slipped a bit more. "Sebastian . . . heeeeelp!"

Sebastian and Holly grabbed Ralphy's legs, but they continued to slip further toward the ledge too. Sebastian's heart gave a horrible jolt. "I don't know what to do!"

"I'm doing all I can!" hollered Ralphy, holding on for dear life.

"Let go of that corn, Mister!" ordered Holly as she took hold of Sebastian's legs.

They were joined by Dasher, Blitzen, and Comet who quickly joined the chain. Everyone tugged.

"Come on everybody!" Sebastian yelled. "Pull hard on three! One . . . two . . . three!"

The entire group pulled with all their might. To Sebastian's relief, they gained several inches, but a second later everyone slipped toward the cliff once again.

"What are we going to do?" Sebastian yelled trying to rack his brain for ideas. He gripped onto Ralphy's legs tighter, pulled harder, and prayed silently for help. Then it hit him, *Hey . . . if Coach Tanner is here, maybe Santa and Donner are nearby too.* Sebastian did the only thing he could think of—*scream!*

"Heeelp! Santa!" Sebastian yelled so loud that it echoed through the mountains.

"You mean to tell me there's a bunch of you but you still can't pull me up?" Tanner asked nastily.

"If you'd just let go of that corn, we *could* pull you up," Ralphy added.

"No! I will . . . not . . . let . . . go!"

"Heeelp! Santaaaa! Help! Help us, please! Santa!" Sebastian's voice echoed through the mountains and was clearly heard by Donner and Santa who had landed and were searching in another area for Coach Tanner. They immediately launched back into the air and followed the sound of Sebastian's voice.

"I'm . . . losing . . . my . . . grip!" Every syllable from Ralphy's mouth trembled as Coach Tanner's hand slowly began to slip away from Ralphy's. "Let go of that corn!" Ralphy begged again.

Sebastian saw the tragedy that was about to happen

and let out one more cry for help. "Santaaaaa! Heeeelp!" He paused. "Coach Tanner, *please l*et go of that corn! Why are you being . . . so . . . stubborn?"

Sebastian wished he could go back in time and change everything. As he held onto Ralphy, his heels were now over his head in the link and all the blood started rushing into his brain.

At that moment, Santa and Donner arrived on the scene. They grabbed hold of the rear of the chain. "Hurry, Donner! Now pull!" said Santa. They heaved and yanked and pulled. Little by little, they inched Tanner closer to safety.

"I can't hold on any longer!" said Ralphy. Sweat poured from his face and continued to drip into the snow beneath him.

Suddenly, Sebastian's Frank Tanner basketball card fell out of his pocket and landed on Tanner's shoulder. The coach gazed at the younger image of himself back in the days when he loved the game. A small smile appeared on Tanner's face.

Sebastian saw the coach gazing at the card. "Did you cheat back then too? Or did you care more about the game then? Did you ever care about your fans like me?" he asked, then paused. "You were my hero."

A gust of wind blew the card off Tanner's shoulder. The coach—and everyone else—watched as it swirled into the air and eventually fell out of sight.

Coach Tanner looked up at Sebastian's inquisitive eyes. "What would your mom want you to do?" Santa shouted.

Coach Tanner looked down at the vast distance between himself and the ground. He didn't know what to say.

"I know you miss your mom, and that's why you're so

angry," Santa said warmly. "I know how much you loved her. But I love you too, Frank, ever since you were a boy. I gave you your first basketball, remember?"

The coach looked at the long string of characters willing to help him. A large tear welled up in his eye. It was that very first basketball that started his love for the game. It was also his favorite present . . . even better than a million dollars and a Learjet.

"I know it was your mom who gave you that beautiful whistle you wear and never take off," said Sebastian.

The whistle was engraved with the coach's initials and birth date.

Coach Tanner remembered the many Christmases he and his mom enjoyed together. He knew that if she could see him now, she would be so disappointed in him. Tears slowly rolled down his cheek as his thoughts drifted back to the baby born on that first Christmas day. As Coach Tanner reflected on the love he felt, he could sense that somehow his burdens had been lifted and deep inside his heart felt light.

Tanner glanced down at the chest of corn that held his dreams and unclenched his fingers.

The chest fell from his hand and disappeared out of sight.

As the group tugged on the coach and began to pull him up, his hand suddenly slipped out of Ralphy's grip. When their hands separated, Ralphy lunged for the coach, but it was too late.

Coach Tanner fell through the air and tumbled down the slopes toward another cliff. At its edge was a drop that looked like it had no end.

"Ralphy! Let's go!" Before anyone could say a word,

Sebastian pushed Ralphy onto his belly and they leapt from their position and landed on the slopes. They took off down the hill on their bellies! They swwwwwished through the snow and slid faster and faster toward the coach like an Olympic bobsled team.

Tanner was rolling down the slope toward eminent destruction, but in a matter of seconds Ralphy and Sebastian were zeroing in on him.

"I'll get us in front of the coach, but we'll only get one pass," Ralphy yelled. "It's up to you to grab him. I need to steer."

Sebastian took a deep breath. He knew he had to think positive. "Just get me in catching range."

Knowing Sebastian's history with catching, Ralphy wished their roles were reversed. He and Sebastian sped down the slope faster and faster. Coach Tanner was only feet away.

Sebastian clamped his legs firmly around Ralphy's neck and leaned forward with his hands outstretched. Then, with a fast, daring maneuver, they skidded in front of the coach. Sebastian lunged forward . . . and . . .

Caught him!

But the weight of Tanner along with the sudden impact pulled Sebastian away. Ralphy grabbed Sebastian by the legs and jammed on his brakes as they slid ever closer toward the cliff's edge.

"Ralphy! Stop us! Quick!" Sebastian yelled.

They started to spin out of control on the icy snow.

Ralphy dug his paw deeper and deeper into the snow to try and stop them, and like a giant snowplow, they began to slow down. Inches from the edge, they finally stopped, completely covered with snow. Six eyes popped out of the icy white, followed by their heads. Everything was silent, until . . .

"You all right, pal?" Ralphy asked.

"Yeah, but I've got a ton of snow in my underwear."

Santa, Holly, and the reindeer cheered from on top of the mountain.

Coach Tanner's face was overwhelmed with emotion. "Thank you! Thank you!" he shouted, snorting with laughter. He hugged Ralphy and Sebastian. "Thank you so much," he said in a sniffly voice. It was the first hug he'd given anyone in years. "You risked your lives for me. Why did you do that?"

"I'd do anything for the great Frank Tanner," admitted Sebastian.

"Oh, come on. You can't still think I'm great anymore."

"I think you could be," replied Sebastian.

The coach paused, thinking, "I'll never forget this . . . Oh no, all that corn . . . Will you still be able to have Christmas?"

"Are you kidding me? shouted Santa from above. "I've got a whole barn full of the stuff back at the Pole! We won't let the children go without Christmas."

Holly chuckled. "He's got a whole barn full? Who knew?" asked Holly.

They all laughed.

Ralphy shook the snow off of his body and embraced Sebastian enthusiastically. "We did it buddy! We did it! What a team we make! That was some catch you made! I knew you'd come through!"

Sebastian sniffed and spit out a mouthful of bear fur. He could hardly be seen in the midst of Ralphy's bear hug.

"Ralphy, please," Sebastian said, "enough with the bear hug. I can't breathe!"

CHAPTER ELEVEN
Rebound

After a quick cell phone call to Santa's Workshop, Dudley sent out several more reindeer to pick everyone up.

It was Christmas Eve and there was a lot of work to be done!

Dudley welcomed Sebastian with a casual handshake, then, overcome with emotion, his true feelings came out and he gave Sebastian a great big hug. The other elves followed, and soon Sebastian and Ralphy were getting more high-fives and hardy pats on the back than they could handle.

Christmas music filled the air. And rightly so—Christmas was only hours away.

One of the elves brought Santa's *big* sleigh out from the barn. The sleigh was fully loaded, complete with leather interior, a Global Positioning System so Santa would never get lost, and an anti-radar detection device created by Spalding so Santa would never be detected.

The elves formed a long assembly line from Santa's Workshop to the sleigh and began loading bags of presents to be delivered by Santa. Bag after bag was handed from one elf to another as they packed the rear of the sleigh.

"What you did was very brave." It was Holly. "I'm so proud of you," she said, beaming.

"Thanks." Sebastian blushed.

The huge smile jumped from Holly's lips to Sebastian's.

Santa was wearing his official red suit. You know, the one he wears every Christmas Eve. He put his arm around Coach Tanner's shoulder. "You were a great player," acknowledged Santa, "one of my favorites. And you *are* a great coach. Most importantly, you are a good boy, Frank."

"Aw, gee . . . thanks, Santa," replied Tanner happily. His smile never left his face. "I want you to know that I'm really sorry for all the trouble I caused. I hope you'll forgive me."

Santa turned to face Tanner. "Already forgiven my friend," he said extending his hand to the coach.

Santa's hand disappeared in Tanner's oversized grip as they shook hands. It caused Santa to burst forth with a hearty belly laugh that only Santa was famous for.

As Sebastian watched Santa and the coach, he remembered something he'd heard Santa say often—that it's the people who are the hardest to love in life that need our love the most. Sebastian saw how love changed Coach Tanner's heart. It was a lesson he'd never forget.

Tanner apologized to Sebastian for all the trouble he caused him too and asked if they could be friends. Sebastian accepted his apology and offered his forgiveness as well.

"We have a lot in common," declared the coach to Sebastian. "I'll tell you what little buddy . . . I'd like to make all of this up to you somehow," Tanner said. "For starters, I want to replace that card you lost, all right?"

"That would be great," Sebastian answered.

"I'll even autograph it for you," Tanner added. "That is . . . if you want me to?" Coach Tanner added humbly.

Sebastian smiled. "I'd like that very much Coach."

Then Tanner picked up the little elf and embraced him. Sebastian and his favorite all-time player were now pals. For Sebastian, it didn't get any better than that.

Dudley also turned to Sebastian and apologized for being a little too hard on him.

"Awww . . . don't sweat it, Dudley old pal." Sebastian waved off the matter with his hand. "You were dealing with the *old* Sebastian, and believe me, this is the *new* me. Besides, I'm really sorry for taking the corn in the first place. I'll be very careful about the decisions I make from now on. No more doing what I'm not supposed to."

"That'll be a relief," Dudley answered plainly.

A beautiful Christmas star appeared overhead in the sky, twinkling majestically above them. The Northern Lights danced all around it.

"Oh, look! It's beautiful," said Sebastian with awe.

Everyone looked up and gazed at the star's beauty.

"Just like the star that led the wise men to the Christ Child," said Santa poignantly, "God's greatest gift of all.

That's why we do this! It's the whole reason that we even have Christmas! So come on, everyone! Christmas Day is almost here!"

Everyone cheered.

The elves continued to load the sleigh with presents as Sebastian picked up a basketball from one of the bags and spun it on his finger. The elves grinned jealously, wishing they could spin a ball like that too.

"That reminds me," said Santa. "With Sebastian wanting to leave us to pursue his dream . . . and my reuniting with Coach Tanner . . . this whole experience made me realize that we work too much around here! In fact, I believe we need to make time in our extremely busy schedules to play and pursue other interests! Because of this, I am designating Sebastian as our first Recreation Director. This is going to be your new job."

"You're *authorizing* play time?" Dudley asked in utter astonishment.

"I am," answered Santa. "I know it's going to help improve our creativity and the quality of our toys!"

The crowd of elves didn't know what to think. They looked bewildered, then shocked, then happy, and they all shouted, "Hooray!"

"Does that mean I can start a basketball league here?" asked Sebastian.

"Yes, of course you can!" answered Santa.

"Basketball?" the elves said.

"Trust me," said Sebastian. "You'll love it."

"Doing something else other than making toys all the time?" asked Wilson. "Hmmm. Give me a ball, baby!"

The elves started cheering.

Suddenly, the ball spun off Sebastian's finger and rolled

out of control toward a pile of presents. It smashed into a big pile of packages ready to be loaded onto Santa's sleigh. The tower of presents wiggled . . . wobbled . . . and fell right on top of Dudley.

"Sebastian!" said Dudley with a hint of frustration, but he still couldn't help himself from smiling.

The large box on the bottom of the pile continued to wiggle. In fact, it seemed to be shaking! Suddenly Jenkins popped out of the box, dizzy, and disoriented. "What a day I'm having," he said, as stars danced around his head.

Everyone laughed, Coach Tanner laughing the loudest of all.

CHAPTER TWELVE
The Gift

Santa began his worldwide journey of delivering presents. The elves were too excited to sleep, so they built Sebastian a special Christmas present. It didn't take them long at all. When he saw the result of their labor, Sebastian couldn't believe his eyes. They had created the most beautiful sight he had ever seen—a basketball court, complete with two hoops, official lines, and bleachers for spectators.

Red and green paint, Santa's favorite colors, decorated the hardwood floor. It was one of the coolest paint jobs anybody had ever seen, even nicer than on any NBA court. Sebastian's name was on a big card attached to the backboard with a giant red bow. Sebastian was speechless.

Dudley cleared his throat. "Do you like it?"

"I love it!" answered Sebastian looking at his friends." Thank you. It's *the best* Christmas present ever."

"Wilson was in charge," said Dudley.

"I used the *actual* North Pole to hold that hoop," said Wilson.

89

They all gazed at the pole. Sure enough—it was The North Pole all right!

"You put that back tomorrow," said Dudley, shaking his head in disbelief. "I'll get you another pole to use."

Everyone laughed.

Cute, funny, silly, awesome, huggable, kind and sometimes naughty are words often used to describe Wilson by his fellow elves. Wilson loves making toys at hyper-speed and snacking on string cheese.

It didn't take Sebastian long to put together some teams and start a game. Of course, Ralphy joined in the fun, too. Coach Tanner stood on the sidelines and gave all the elves some tips. Basketball was new to the elves, but they took to it very quickly. Their can-do spirit and positive attitude helped a lot, no matter what they were doing. "Okay elf people! Have some fun out there!" the coach exclaimed. He turned to Wilson. "I love these elves." Then he turned his attention back to Sebastian. "You know, I think it's time you got in the game and played too."

"Me?"

"Yeah, you," Coach Tanner insisted.

"All right!" Sebastian ran onto the court. As he jogged

past Holly, she grabbed him by the arm and looked deep into his eyes. "Put that ball through the hoop. You may be an elf, but you're six feet tall in my heart." She leaned in and kissed him on the cheek.

Sebastian's temperature rose and his heart beat fast like a drum. Inside, he was exploding like fireworks! Then Sebastian composed himself and jogged onto the court to play ball. "She sure can talk basketball," he said to himself. "Man, if only I could get above the rim."

Sebastian stopped in his tracks. He imagined himself running into the stable and opening the chest of feed corn. *No. No way! What was I thinking?* Sebastian stopped that thought immediately.

It didn't take long for the ball to be passed to him. Sebastian made great passes and hit fade-away jump shots from three-point range. The elves in the bleachers—and Holly—cheered him on.

"Hey, how'd you like to come back to Polarville with me?" Coach Tanner asked Sebastian. "The point guard position could be all yours."

"Really?" Sebastian exclaimed, but paused when he noticed the look on all of the elves' faces. He turned back to Tanner and said, "Gee, thanks Coach, but this is my home team. This is where I belong."

"You scared me for a second there," Ralphy confessed.

"Me, too," Holly added.

"That reminds me!" Tanner gasped. "*My* team! I gotta get back. We play the All Stars tomorrow."

"Don't worry," said Ralphy. "We can get you back there first thing in the morning. Besides, you already know how to ride a reindeer."

A burst of laughter came from Sebastian. Then he

grabbed the basketball and resumed the game. Dudley guarded him closely. Sebastian chuckled at the fact that Dudley actually thought he could compete with him. He casually looked into the stands as he dribbled and locked eyes with Holly. She smiled "that smile" and his heart skipped a beat. He felt more courageous than ever.

"Sebastian! Sebastian! Sebastian!" Everyone began chanting his name.

Desire filled Sebastian's eyes.

"Take it to him!" Coach Tanner shouted.

Sebastian's smile grew wider and he took off down the court! Dudley stayed with him, matching his every step. Sebastian faked left, then right, then dribbled the ball behind his back and bolted for the hoop. He left Dudley in the dust.

I'm going to dunk this basketball, thought Sebastian. His mind searched for a creative way to do it. He dribbled down to Ralphy and ran up his polar bear friend's back to the basket and executed a trademark Frank Tanner Super Duper Dunk.

Coach Tanner applauded as the other elves exploded with cheers.

"Elves *can* dunk," laughed Sebastian.

". . . with a little help," chuckled Ralphy.

THE END

POST GAME
Report

> **Brought to you by Sully's Snow Cones, the best tasting snow cones at the North Pole.**

Dear Reader,

While that first North Pole basketball game with the elves was going on, Spalding had Jenkins in his laboratory and was teaching him a lesson. He made Jenkins wear the "official" elf candy cane striped overalls and write, "I will be good" over and over again on a blackboard. Spalding had a whole series of additional activities planned for Jenkins—everything from elf singing to elf baking was included. Jenkins would certainly be a new (and good) man when Spalding was through with him.

Frank Tanner went back to Polarville and coached a winning season, his first in four years. He was named "Coach of the Year" and everyone knew the reason for his success—he had rediscovered his love for the game. Coach Tanner also lived with the spirit of Christmas in his life every day. May that be truly said of us all!

Coach Tanner, Sebastian, and Santa remained close friends and kept in touch regularly with phone calls and e-mails. Together they made plans to help needy children throughout the world with charity basketball games on Christmas Day that even Santa played in. As for the magic reindeer corn . . . well, Santa moved that to a safe hiding place at the North Pole. It's ready and waiting for next Christmas when Santa hitches up his team of flying reindeer to visit *you*. So don't forget to be good and love one another.

Robert Skead

Check out these other books by Robert Skead:

Elves Can't Tackle
Elves Can't Kick
Patriots, Redcoats & Spies
Submarines, Secrets & a Daring Rescue
Something to Prove:
    The Great Satchel Paige vs. the Rookie Joe DiMaggio
Safe at Home: a baseball card mystery
Hitting Glory: a baseball bat adventure
Mighty Mike Bounces Back

Attention All Elves! Santa's North Pole Court Basketball Tips

- There's no tickling in basketball. Ever.

- When you shoot an air ball, stop pretending it was a bad pass.

- Climbing up on each other's shoulders to block a shot is fun, but illegal.

- Flying reindeer are for guiding Santa's sleigh, not for acrobatic slam dunking.

- Don't tickle an opposing player when their hands are up in the air guarding you. See Number 1.

- Always let Santa win. A happy Santa means you keep your job. LOL

Check out book two in the series!

ELVES CAN'T
TACKLE!
ROBERT SKEAD

Sebastian and the gang are on a mission to give Jack Fabulous, professional football's most famous quarterback, a little Christmas spirit. In the process, Sebastian ends up on the team for the Christmas Eve "Sandwich Bowl" game. But there is a huge problem—Sebastian is an elf – and *Elves Can't Tackle!*